We Feel Good Out Here

Zhik gwaa'an,
nakhwatthąįįtat
gwiinzìi

Fifth House Ltd.
A Fitzhenry & Whiteside
Company
1511, 1800-4 St. SW
Calgary, Alberta T2S 2S5

1-800-387-9776
www.fitzhenry.ca

THE CANADA COUNCIL | LE CONSEIL DES ARTS
FOR THE ARTS | DU CANADA
SINCE 1957 | DEPUIS 1957

CANADIAN NORTH
seriously northern

CIBC

© **Mixed Sources**
Product group from well-managed
forests and other controlled sources
www.fsc.org Cert no. SW-COC-1271
© 1996 Forest Stewardship Council
FSC

First published in the
United States in 2008 by
Fitzhenry & Whiteside
311 Washington Street
Brighton, Massachusetts,
02135

Cover and interior design by John Luckhurst
Frontispiece map by Toby Foord
Photography by Tessa Macintosh
Additional photographs by Lawrence Norbert (Khaii luk, p.7), Bruce Bowls (Julie-Ann as a child, p.9),
Alestine Andre (spruce gum and dwarf labrador p.11), Mindy Willett (kids kissing mom, p.20)

Edited by Meaghan Craven
Proofread by Michelle Lomberg

The type in this book is set in 10-on-15 point Trebuchet Regular and 10-on-13 point Tekton Oblique.

The publisher gratefully acknowledges the support of The Canada Council for the Arts and the
Department of Canadian Heritage.

We acknowledge the financial support of the Government of Canada through the Book Publishing
Industry Development Program (BPIDP) for our publishing activities.

The authors would like to thank Canadian North, CIBC, the Gwich'in Land Use Planning Board
(GLUPB), the NWT Protected Areas Strategy Secretariat, and WWF-Canada for financial assistance
in the completion of this book.

Printed in Canada by Friesens on Forest Stewardship Council (FSC) Approved paper

2008 / 1

Library and Archives Canada Cataloguing in Publication

André, Julie-Ann
We feel good out here = Zhik gwaa'an, nakhwatthaiitat gwiinzii /
Julie-Ann André and Mindy Willett; photographs by Tessa Macintosh.

(Land is our storybook) Includes text in Gwich'in.

ISBN 978-1-897252-33-8

1. André, Julie-Ann—Juvenile literature. 2. André, Julie-Ann— Family—Juvenile literature.
3. Gwich'in Indians—Northwest Territories—Juvenile literature. 4. Traditional ecological knowledge—
Northwest Territories—Juvenile literature. 5. Gwich'in Indians—Northwest Territories—Tsiigehtchic—
Biography—Juvenile literature. 6. Tsiigehtchic (N.W.T.)—Biography—Juvenile literature. I. Willett,
Mindy, 1968- II. Title. III. Series.

E99.K84A64 2008   j971.9'30049720092   C2008-900421-3

Acknowledgements

We would like to thank: Susan Mackenzie (land use planner) and the Gwich'in Land Use Planning Board, Pete Ewins of WWF-Canada, the NWT Protected Areas Strategy Secretariat, and CIBC for their financial contributions; the community of Tsiigehtchic for their hospitality; Alestine Andre and William Firth of the Gwich'in Social and Cultural Institute for translations and Alestine for sharing her spruce medicine and for her dedication to the preservation of Gwich'in culture; Jamie Bastedo, Judith Drinnan, and Karen Hamre for their ongoing encouragement and support; Dot van Vliet for her initial design that helped us realize the dream; Tom Andrews, Alestine Andre and Ingrid Kritsch, Gladys Norwegian, and John Stewart for reviewing the transcript; Julie-Ann André's family, including Amanda and Anna May, Julie-Ann's dad, Gabe, Julie-Ann's mother, Rosa, and brothers, Robert, Donald, and Danny, for all their traditional knowledge; Randy for encouraging and supporting Julie-Ann to keep up with her traditional habits; Mindy's family, Damian, Jack, and Rae Panayi, for their ongoing love; Charlene Dobmeier and Meaghan Craven from Fifth House for taking on this large project; and especially Tessa for the incredible journey together making this book become a reality.

To Anna-May and Amanda and all future generations. May they all find the strengths of their ancestors and take the opportunity to learn their culture and history.

We Feel Good Out Here

Out Here

Zhik gwaa'an, nakhwatthaiitat gwiinzii

By **JULIE-ANN ANDRÉ** and **MINDY WILLETT**

Photographs by **Tessa Macintosh**

FIFTH
HOUSE

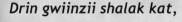

Drin gwiinzii shalak kat,

My name is Julie-Ann André. I'm a *Gwichya Gwich'in* woman from Tsiigehtchic in the Northwest Territories. I want to share my family's story and the story of our land—*Khaii luk*, the land of winter fish. It's a small part of Gwich'in traditional lands.

The land has a story to tell, if you know how to listen. When I travel, the land tells me where my ancestors have been. It tells me where the animals have come and gone, and it tells me what the weather may be like tomorrow.

I feel good out here.

The land is an important part of who I am.

Being out, doing what my people have always done—boating, travelling, trapping, fishing, hunting, surviving, and enjoying what the land provides—helps me to teach my children and others about our culture. That's important to me.

Come along with me, meet my family, and listen to our story...

Julie-Ann André

Meet my daughters, Anna-May and Amanda, and my husband, Randy Niditchie. We live in Tsiigehtchic on the *Tsiigehnjik* and *Nagwichoonjik* Rivers. These rivers and the land they flow through are full of stories.

In the earliest days of history, called *ts'ii deii* days, our stories tell us about the journeys of *Atachuukaii* and other leaders. *Atachuukaii* was known as a great traveller and warrior. The adventures of his life are told in stories, including his fight with the giant *Ch'ii choo*.

In the *ts'ii deii* days *Deetrin'*, the raven trickster, would talk with *Atachuukaii* about the colours Raven had given to the animals. That *Deetrin'* could talk didn't surprise anyone, as these were the days when animals and humans could change form, speak with one another, and were equals. The stories about *Deetrin'* and *Atachuukaii* tell us how the land got its shape, how animals got their colours, and much more.

Anna-May, Julie-Ann, Amanda, and Randy—the André-Niditchie family.

2

Our Stories: *Deetrin'*

Raven is known as a trickster and for his magic powers. He loved to play tricks on the other animals. His tricks sometimes caused the animals' appearances to change. One time, Raven lied and told the grebes that some members of their family had died. They started to mourn. To show how sad they were and to spare the spirits of the dead, they jumped in and out of a fire. Their long golden hair became singed and brown, and that is the way it is to this day.

This is how my dad tells the story about how *Atachuukaii* caused the death of the giant *Ch'ii Choo*. He shares how *Atachuukaii's* adventures shaped our land.

Our Stories *Ch'ii choo* Chases *Atachuukaii* up *Nagwichoonjik*

On this side of Fort Yukon, they say, there are lots of islands in the river. That's where the giant *Ch'ii choo* started chasing *Atachuukaii*. He followed him all the way from there to here; they passed through here and over there, and up the river. One old man in Fort Good Hope told me that when they passed the Ramparts on the Mackenzie River, *Atachuukaii* left his canoe—it is still there. It's now a rock turned upside down.

From there *Atachuukaii* ran ashore. The giant ran along this side of the river, still following him. He took six steps and created six big lakes between Norman Wells and Fort Good Hope. *Ch'ii choo* stopped chasing *Atachuukaii* when he finally starved to death because of *Atachuukaii's* cleverness. Here's how it happened.

Every time *Ch'ii choo* killed good things to eat, he cooked them real good. But then he would go and have a good wash before eating the food. Well, every time *Ch'ii choo* went to wash up, *Atachuukaii* sent many animals in to clean up what *Ch'ii choo* was going to eat. So *Ch'ii choo* never had anything to eat.

At last, the giant cut a piece of his own backside off and made pemmican from it. He should have eaten it right there! Instead, he said, "I wonder who can freeze it for me?" *Atachuukaii* overheard this, and when he saw a muskrat swim by, he said to the rat, "Why don't you go over there and freeze that grease?" (That's what they called pemmican, grease.)

The rat went over to *Ch'ii choo* and said, "There's a creek over here with cold water. I'll freeze it for you." So *Ch'ii choo* gave the grease to the rat, and the rat swam over into the creek. *Atachuukaii* was sitting there. He took a little rock and threw it at the rat, hitting him in the mouth. The rat let go of the grease, and it floated down the river. *Atachuukaii* went down to where the rat was swimming, and he scooped the grease and some water up with both hands, and he drank it. Since that time, people drink water in that way. They scoop it up with two hands.

The rat went back to *Ch'ii choo* and told him, "I lost that grease. It all fell in the water." That's when *Ch'ii choo* started crying and singing about sunrise and sunset, and how he'd never see them again. Then, at last, he starved to death. That's how *Atachuukaii* was able to beat *Ch'ii choo*. That's what was told to me by the old people.

All references throughout this book to *Atachuukaii* and *Deetrin'* come from *Googwandak: The History and Stories of the Gwichya Gwich'in* by Michael Heine, Alestine Andre, Ingrid Kritsch, Alma Cardinal, and the Elders of Tsiigehtchic (Gwich'in Social and Cultural Institute, 2001).

The Ramparts River and Wetlands area includes a critical wetland for waterfowl and is home to two species at risk, the peregrine falcon and boreal woodland caribou. The Ramparts figure in the stories and culture of the Sahtu Dene people, as well as the Gwich'in people.

My family's favourite place is *Khaii luk*, which means, "winter fish." We call it that because there are always fish here in every season.

My family has been using this area for hunting and fishing for many, many years. I also trap here for marten, mink, wolverine, and wolf, just as my father and mother did before me. We also hunt for caribou, which usually migrate by *Khaii luk* in the late winter or early spring.

To make sure that our land and its animals are healthy, my family has worked hard to preserve and protect the *Khaii luk* area. My dad's stories and knowledge about his life on the land helped to develop the Gwich'in Land Use Plan, which includes *Khaii luk* in a Conservation Zone (see the map on page 24). Our land use plan is the first in the Northwest Territories to be complete. The plan ensures that some land is open for development, and it protects our special places. We want to make sure that all users, especially industry, respect the land so that future generations may enjoy it.

I am sharing my dad's stories with my daughters. They're growing up knowing their people and culture and the land that nurtures us.

Our Words

English	Gwichya Gwich'in
Beaver	*Tse'*
Black duck	*Njaa*
Canada goose	*Kheh*
Caribou	*Vadzaih*
Lake trout	*Vit*
Moose	*Dinjik*
Muskrat	*Dzan*
Porcupine	*Ts'it*
Snowy owl	*Vihsaiivee*

Julie-Ann with Susan Mackenzie, planner with the Gwich'in Land Use Planning Board.

Right: Khaii luk. Try and find it on the map.

Gabe Andre, Julie-Ann's dad, sharing knowledge with his daughter and granddaughters.

I was raised in the *Khaii luk* area. My family moved around between *Khaii luk*, Big Lake, and across *Nugwichoonjik* from *Duchun choo gehnjik*. We trapped, fished, and lived off the land. It was such a great place to grow up because I had all the freedom in the world.

When I was only seven years old, I was picked up in an airplane and taken to residential school. When I was there, I had to do what I was told, and I had to speak English. It was very formal—do this, do that, line up, feel this, think that. Life at the residential school townized me so much that I was no longer comfortable in my own culture or with who I was. I wasn't allowed to speak my language or see my family. When I grew older and went home, I felt completely out of place and lost.

I've worked hard the last ten years to unlearn a lot of what I learned at residential school and to get my cultural practices and beliefs back. I have learned how to hunt and trap on my own and to always listen to my Elders when they talk. I am also trying to work on my language, but it makes me very angry that I can't speak to my parents in Gwich'in.

Julie-Ann before going to residential school.

It will take a while for me to feel that I am truly a part of my home again, but I'm getting there, and I'm bringing my family along with me on the journey.

When we are in Tsiigehtchic, my daughters go to the Chief Paul Niditchie School. They need to get a good education so that they can live their dreams.

The school in Tsiigehtchic is named after Randy Niditchie's grandfather.

This year I'm going to school in Inuvik, studying business management at Aurora College. I want to run my own cultural tourism business to share the land with others.

Another important form of school for me is with a different kind of teacher, my cousin, Alestine. She knows a lot about our culture. When she talks, I put up my "antennae ears" and listen very carefully to what she says. For example, she's taught me about traditional medicines such as the spruce tree and dwarf labrador.

Julie-Ann with Alestine. Alestine is older than Julie-Ann. Their dads are brothers. Alestine speaks and understands Gwichya Gwich'in and earned an interdisciplinary master's degree from the University of Victoria. Alestine works for the Gwich'in Cultural and Social Institute (GCSI), which documents, preserves, and promotes the practice of Gwich'in culture, language, and traditional knowledge and values.

Gwich'in medicine makers say the best medicines are made from Ts'eevii (black spruce). The tree's cones, boughs, inner bark, and gum are used. Julie-Ann holds spruce gum in her hands, which is used to soothe irritated skin and reduce infection.

The Gwich'in people use the stems, leaves, and tops of Lidii maskeg (dwarf labrador) to make tea for colds and clearing nasal passages. This plant is available year round, even under the snow.

While I'm in school, we live in Inuvik. Anna-May and Amanda enjoy the big town and go to a big school. They love to go to the pool in Inuvik as they don't get that chance in Tsiigehtchic. But, come summer, they are happy to head back home so we can go boating and enjoy our family and the quiet of our bush camp.

Julie-Ann wants her kids to know how to swim, as they spend a lot of time boating in the summer. She takes them to the Inuvik Family Centre.

The girls love to watch Scooby-Dooby-Doo on their TV DVD.

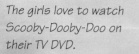

INUVIK FAMILY CENTRE

The André-Niditchie family enjoys breakfast at their home in Inuvik.

To help them learn their culture, and just to have fun, I take my daughters out trapping and fishing with me.

Sometimes they complain and say, "Ah, but Mom do I have to?" I always explain that for them to know who they are they must know the land and the animals that live on it.

Julie-Ann is recognizable in her red sweatshirt as a Canadian Ranger. She is a sergeant and helps run the Junior Ranger program. The Canadian Rangers are part of the Canadian Forces and are often called "the eyes and ears in the north."

To get to the trapline,
Amanda and Anna-May ride
on the back of the toboggan.

The first thing we do when we are on the land is set up camp. Then, we set snares and traps, collect snow for tea, and gather wood for the fire. We care for the animals in the proper way; we check our traps regularly to show our respect for the animals and to make sure trapped animals do not suffer or get eaten by other animals. We are always grateful for the life they give.

I teach my daughters how to set snares for rabbits (*geh*) and about their habits and stories. *Geh* have always been important to my people for food and clothing.

When I was growing up, I was told that *geh* like to dance. You can see big round trails or beaten paths on sandbars—these marks are left by the *geh* dancing. There is a traditional Gwich'in dance performed with fiddle and guitar called the rabbit dance.

Our Words

English	Gwichya Gwich'in
Fox	*Naagadh*
Lynx	*Niinjii*
Marten	*Tsuk*
Mink	*Chihthee*
Rabbit (hare)	*Geh*
Wolverine	*Nehtryuh*

I trap *naagadh*, *geh*, *tsuk*, *niinjii*, *nehtryuh*, and *chihthee* in the winter. The trapping season ends at the end of February when mating season begins. The fur is used to make clothing for ourselves or to sell. Some animals we eat. The unused parts are disposed of in different ways. We believe it is not respectful to the animals to just discard their carcasses, so most people will bury them, burn them, or feed them to their dogs.

The highset trap is used for animals such as marten and mink.

Julie-Ann is proud of the fox and marten she has trapped. She will either sell the fur or use it to make mittens or a hat. The fur is much better than anything store-bought to keep warm in the northern winters.

Julie-Ann teaches Amanda and Anna-May how to set a snare for rabbits. A snare is a wire noose that you can hardly see (look for it between the willows). She teaches them to look for tracks, droppings, and chewed willows and to put a snare on one of the rabbit's trails. If the snare is set properly, a rabbit caught in it will die quickly, won't suffer, and as a result the meat will taste good.

We all have to work hard when we're out on the land. One of the biggest tasks is to gather the *ah'* to sleep on. *Ah'* is the Gwich'in word for spruce boughs. We cut them off the spruce trees to make a woven mat on the ground that keeps us warm when we sleep.

I wish you could smell how beautiful it is. It's like the fresh smell of Christmas trees in the tent.

When I was little, my mother used to tell me that *Muskrew* would come and take me away if I stayed up late. I would get so scared when I heard him hoot! I know my mother said this to make sure I went to bed early, but I don't want my kids to get scared, so I tell them that *Muskrew* is just an owl.

At night, when we're on the land, I share the stories my father used to tell me, such as those of *Atachuukaii*. There is a place far, far from here in the Ramparts on *Nagwichoonjik* where he laid down his canoe; you can still see the landmark. One waterfall is known as the place where *Atachuukaii* had a pee. I took my girls to this place by boat one summer. It was fun to show them how our land is our storybook.

My daughters never want to go back to town once we're out here. Out on the land there is no TV, and they have to entertain themselves.

Amanda entertains herself by playing the "drums" on the kitchen pots. Her drumsticks are kindling for the fire, which is used to heat the tent.

Their dad often reads the bedtime stories. Their favourites include Archie comic books. Amanda also likes books about science and why things are the way they are. Anna-May likes all books about animals.

20

When we leave *Khaii luk* to go back to town, we always leave an offering for the spirits. This gesture is to say thank you to the land and to pay our respects. We feel so good out here that we want to make sure the land stays healthy.

Remember *Atachuukaii* the traveller? It is said that he has been travelling beyond the boundaries of the known world for longer than anyone now living can remember. It is also said that the world will not come to an end before he returns from those distant parts.

This land has many stories to tell and many more that have not yet been told. Not all the stories that began during *ts'ii deii* days have ended yet.

By knowing both about the land and the modern world, my children will be able to make sure that the land continues to tell its story. They will know how to listen.

All the Details!

Atachuukaii – Great Gwich'in traveller, leader, and medicine man.

Ch'ii choo – One of the giants in Gwich'in stories.

Deetrin' – Raven. Known as a trickster.

Drin gwiinzii shalak kat – "Good day, my friends."

Gwich'in Land Use Planning – People plan the use of land to keep track of how an area should be used. Land use plans are guides for future activities. The plan considers traditional uses of the land, transportation, garbage disposal, military activities, mining, timber, oil and gas, tourism, fisheries, and many more activities. The plan strives to strike a balance between conservation of land and people's use of land, water, and resources. The map on this page shows what is allowed and not allowed in specific areas, or zones. There are four zones: General Use (where all land uses are possible), Special Management (where all uses are possible if certain conditions are met), and Conservation and Heritage Conservation (where commercial development is not allowed).

Gwich'in language – *Dinjii Zhu' Ginjik* (Gwich'in language) is one of the most endangered Aboriginal languages in Canada. Because English is spoken in daily life, only a small number of Elders and a few others continue to speak the language regularly.

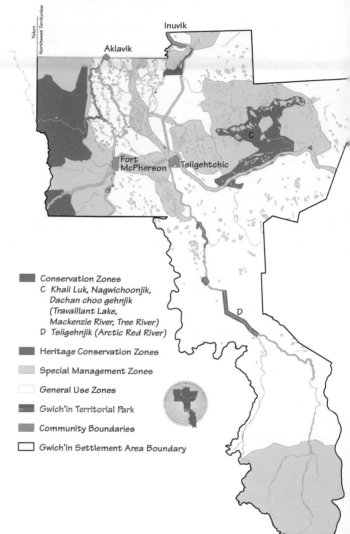

Conservation Zones
C Khaii Luk, Nagwichoonjik, Dachan choo gehnjik (Travaillant Lake, Mackenzie River, Tree River)
D Tsiigehnjik (Arctic Red River)

Heritage Conservation Zones

Special Management Zones

General Use Zones

Gwich'in Territorial Park

Community Boundaries

Gwich'in Settlement Area Boundary

Gwich'in Land Use Map - *Courtesy Nành' Geenjit Gwitr'it Tigwaa'in (Working for the Land), the Gwich'in Land Use Plan, Gwich'in Land Use Planning Board, 2003.*

Nasalization of vowels is common in the Gwichya Gwich'in dialect. Nasal vowels are made when air is pushed through the nose, giving the vowel a nasal or "n" sound. These kinds of vowels are marked by a little hook underneath the letter. To find out more, go to the Gwich'in Social and Cultural Institute (GSCI) website, www.gwichin.ca

Gwichya Gwich'in – The Gwichya Gwich'in are a group of Gwich'in people that mostly live in the Tsiigehtchic area. They are called the "people of the flat land" and are the most easterly group of the Gwich'in people of the North.

"The land" – When Julie-Ann talks about the land, she means much more than just land. She means the air, water, land, and all the parts of the natural world that combine to make up where she comes from. "The land" is another way of saying "home."

Nagwichoonjik – Gwich'in name for the river now known as the Mackenzie, after Alexander Mackenzie (who only visited it for a short while). Each Dene language group has their own name for the great river.

Residential Schools – The first residential schools in the NWT were set up before Confederation. By the mid- to late 1800s, the federal government began to fund the schools. By 1920, most children aged seven to fifteen attended. Students stayed in residences. Some had no contact with their families for up to ten months at a time, some for many years. They weren't allowed to speak their language and were often punished for doing so.

Ts'ii deii **days** – The Gwichya Gwich'in believe that there was a time in the history of the land when animals could change into human form. They are familiar with the habits of the animals upon which they have depended for their survival for as long as they can remember. However, there are places on the land where animals, or other beings, have left marks and tracks that are unlike any that the Gwichya Gwich'in have seen during their travels on the land. These marks and tracks show that the beings that left them must have been huge! These giant animals, *chijuudiee*, have inhabited the land since the earliest days, and some of them may be living there still. One of these giants was *Ch'ii choo*, which Gabe Andre described in the story on page 4.

Tsiigehnjik – Gwich'in name for the Arctic Red River.

About the Authors and Photographer

Julie-Ann André recently graduated from college with a diploma in management studies and started her own cultural tourism business called, Timber Island Enterprises. She takes people out to experience the beautiful land and Gwich'in culture and history.

Mindy Willett is an educator living in Yellowknife. She enjoys her work in the north so much that she often pinches herself to make sure it's real. When she isn't pinching herself, she can be found paddling or skiing on Great Slave Lake with her young family.

Tessa Macintosh first came north to Cape Dorset in 1974. A few years later she headed to Yellowknife to work as a photographer for the *Native Press* and then the NWT government. She is now a freelance photographer living in Yellowknife. Her favourite experiences are with people out on the land.